BATTLE OF THE BEAUTIES

FRIGG

VS

APHRODITE

by Lydia Lukidis

CAPSTONE PRESS
a capstone imprint

Published by Capstone Press, an imprint of Capstone.
1710 Roe Crest Drive, North Mankato, Minnesota 56003
capstonepub.com

Library of Congress Cataloging-in-Publication Data is available on the Library of Congress website
ISBN: 9781669016267 (hardcover)
ISBN: 9781669016212 (paperback)
ISBN: 9781669016229 (ebook PDF)

Summary:
Who will win this battle of famous beauty? In Asgard, the Norse goddess Frigg rules over marriage, motherhood, family, and prophecy. Meanwhile, the Greek goddess Aphrodite reigns over love, beauty, and fertility. In this battle between two powerful ancient goddesses, who will come out on top?

Editorial Credits
Editor: Aaron Sautter; Designer: Bobbie Nuytten; Media Researcher: Rebekah Hubstenberger; Production Specialist: Whitney Schaefer

Image Credits
Alamy: Chronicle, 7, 17, 19, 25, Historic Images, 27, Lebrecht Music & Arts, 4, SPCOLLECTION; 15, Bridgeman Images: 11; Dreamstime: Volodymyr Polotovskyi, 8; Getty Images: Aleksej Arestov/EyeEm, 22, Grafissimo, 23, iStock/LeniKovaleva, 9, Photos.com, 21, iStock/Stanislav Chegleev, cover (bottom right), 5, 29; Shutterstock: Prokrida, cover (top left), 28, Ruslana Stovner, 13; The Metropolitan Museum of Art: The Elisha Whittelsey Collection, The Elisha Whittelsey Fund, 1966, 12

Printed and bound in China. PO5379

TABLE OF CONTENTS

Words in **bold** are in the glossary.

THE QUEEN VS. THE OLYMPIAN

A light mist hovers above the ground. A woman sits on a throne, holding a commanding pose. She wears a long robe the color of the sky.

All hail Frigg! She's the most important goddess of the Norse **pantheon.** She is a mighty queen who rules beside her husband, Odin, the Allfather.

Frigg is the goddess of motherhood and running the household. But her duties don't end there. She's also in charge of marriage, childbirth, and **fertility**.

Frigg

FACT

There are many similarities between the Norse goddesses Frigg and Freya. In fact, some historians believe they are the same goddess.

CHIRP, CHIRP!

A dozen sparrows whoosh through the air, lugging a chariot. A beautiful goddess steers it.

Welcome, Aphrodite! She's one of the twelve **Olympians** in Greek mythology. Aphrodite is one busy goddess. She's in charge of love and beauty, fertility, marriage, and **procreation.** She also has a special connection to the sea.

Aphrodite is very graceful, but she's also one tough cookie. She has both a kind and a destructive side.

Which of these gifted goddesses is more powerful? Who has more abilities? Frigg and Aphrodite will have to battle it out. Who will come out on top?

Aphrodite

DIVINE BEGINNINGS

Frigg is a mysterious goddess. We don't know much about her origins. Historians aren't even sure who her family is.

Some ancient Norse texts say she's the daughter of Fjorgynn—a male giant with godly powers. He represents the earth. Like Odin, Frigg probably comes from a line of giants. In Norse mythology, the giants were the first beings. They existed even before the gods.

As for Frigg's mother, nobody really knows who she is. But we do know that Frigg's name means "beloved" or "dear."

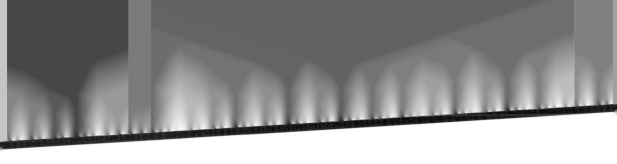

The giant Ymir was the first being to appear in Norse mythology. The race of giants was born from his body.

Venus

FACT

The Birth of Venus is a famous painting that artist Sandro Botticelli created in 1485. The Roman goddess Venus is based on Aphrodite, so this painting also references Aphrodite.

How did Aphrodite come to be? Actually, there are two stories about her birth. The first is pretty normal. In Greek myths, her father is Zeus, king of the gods. Her mother is Dione, an ancient **Titaness.** This makes Aphrodite a second-generation goddess, like most Olympians.

But the Greek poet Hesiod weaves a more incredible tale. He says Aphrodite's birth began with the titan Cronus. Cronus wanted to be the big boss, so he killed his father, Uranus. According to the myths, Uranus was the original god of the heavens.

Then, SPLOOSH! Cronus tossed Uranus's body into the sea. Then a foam began to appear in the water. Next thing you know, a scallop shell rose up from the foam. Aphrodite then emerged from the shell wearing no clothes. The story fits. After all, the Greek word "aphros" means "sea foam."

One story says Aphrodite first appeared from the ocean riding on a large seashell.

Frigg has many strengths. She's best known for her fierce dedication as a loving mother. Mothers give life and unconditional love.

Frigg has two children; twin sons Baldur and Hodr. She would do anything for them. One famous Norse tale shows her devotion. One night, Baldur had a nightmare that predicted his death. Frigg had the same nightmare. But she was determined to prevent her son's death.

She used her powers and authority to make all things in creation, living and nonliving, promise to never harm her son. She visited giants and gods. She talked to animals and plants. She even made elements and objects such as fire, water, stones, and weapons promise her son's safety. Unfortunately, Baldur died anyway. But Frigg never gave up trying to save him.

Frigg called on all living and nonliving things to protect her son Baldur.

Aphrodite's main strength can be summed up in one word: love. As the goddess of love, countless gods and **mortal** men admire her. With just one glance, she can make others fall head over heels for her.

But she's not just incredibly beautiful. She also owns a magical **girdle**. It makes the person wearing it irresistible. She can make others fall in love and desire one another too. For example, she helped spark the love between the Greek hero Jason and Medea, the daughter of the Colchian King.

Neither the gods nor mortal men could resist Aphrodite's beauty.

Aphrodite isn't just the goddess of love and desire. She also oversees marriage, fertility, and childbirth. She helps others come together to create a strong family.

FACT

Aphrodite's son, Eros, is also in charge of love. Eros is a god but looks more like a young boy with wings. He's similar to Cupid from Roman mythology.

Eros

Frigg isn't just a loving mother. She has many other strengths. Intelligence? Check. A strong will and an independent spirit? Check and check. She's a supportive wife to Odin, too. But make no mistake, she's not his servant. She's his equal.

In Norse myths, Frigg is the only person other than Odin allowed to sit on his throne. And, even though Odin is the Norse god of wisdom, Frigg can outsmart him. In one tale, Frigg and Odin bet on which prince will make a better King, Agnar or Geirröth. Frigg outwitted her husband and won.

Like Aphrodite, Frigg is also a goddess of fertility and marriage. She often arranges marriages and protects families. She also helps women in childbirth. In one ancient poem, Frigg uses special plants and herbs to help women have their babies.

Marshland Queen

In Norse mythology, Frigg is very independent. In fact, she doesn't always live with her husband Odin. She often stays in the foggy, watery realm of Fensalir, which means "hall of the marshlands." All marshy and swampy grounds are special to Frigg.

Love isn't Aphrodite's only power. Her other main strength is her stunning beauty. Thanks to her perfect body and face, she enchants all those who look her way. She also has the power to grant beauty and charms to others.

Beauty may not seem very powerful, but think again. Because of her beauty, Aphrodite can influence others. In a famous myth, Zeus asked the mortal man, Paris, to decide who was most beautiful—Aphrodite, Hera, or Athena. Of course, Aphrodite won.

Before Paris picked Aphrodite in the beauty contest, she had promised him the love of the most beautiful mortal woman, Helen. But Helen was married to King Menelaus of Sparta. Aphrodite helped Paris kidnap Helen and bring her to Troy. Her actions helped spark the Trojan War.

Paris chose Aphrodite as the most beautiful of all the goddesses.

AWESOME POWERS

Like Odin, Frigg has certain powers when it comes to magic. In an ancient manuscript found in Germany, Frigg is shown using magic to heal a horse.

Frigg also has the power of **divination**. She can see into the future and is known as a "seer." Before Baldur died, she had a vivid dream that predicted his death.

As a sky goddess and master weaver, Frigg weaves the clouds that produce rain to help crops grow. She also weaves the magical threads of fate, known as *Wyrd*, in a similar way.

FACT

Frigg first appeared in Marvel comics as Thor's mother, and Loki's adoptive mother, in 1963. She was later an important part of the first two Thor movies.

Spin Master

As a homemaker, Frigg takes pride in her skill at spinning wool. In many myths, she uses the wool of the cloud sheep to weave and spin garments for the gods. Many women call on her when they need help spinning wool. As a goddess of the sky, Frigg also spins and weaves the clouds themselves.

Step aside Frigg, you're not the only powerful one. Aphrodite also has great power—the power of creation. Pygmalion was a famous sculptor. He created a statue of a woman so beautiful that he fell in love with it. He begged Aphrodite to turn the statue into a real woman. Aphrodite agreed, then, POOF! She brought the statue to life.

Aphrodite also played a role in the creation of the first mortal woman, Pandora. The gods formed Pandora out of clay. Then Aphrodite gifted her with beauty that made her powerful and desired by others.

Aphrodite can even help protect her favorite warriors. She saved Paris when he was about to be killed during the Trojan War. She wrapped him in a cloud that carried him back home.

Pandora

Aphrodite has another handy superpower—immortality. This goddess will live forever. As for Frigg, her fate is unclear. Many Norse gods will die during Ragnarök. At this final battle nearly all mortal people and gods will die.

But Frigg and Aphrodite do have one other power in common; the ability to **shapeshift**. Frigg can turn herself into a bird using a pair of magical falcon **plumes**.

Frigg's magical feathers gave her the ability to take the form of a bird.

Aphrodite can take the form of various creatures. In one myth, the monster Typhon descended upon Mount Olympus. He threatened to attack the gods and goddesses. As he approached Aphrodite, she escaped by turning herself into a fish.

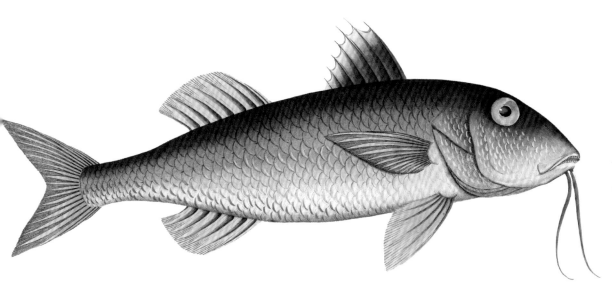

When necessary, Aphrodite could turn into creatures such as a fish.

FLAWED GODDESSES

Although Frigg is powerful and a devoted mother, she can't save Baldur. Loki, a trickster god in Norse mythology, tricked her. Frigg had asked everything in creation to help protect Baldur. However, she didn't ask the mistletoe plant. She thought it was small and harmless. But Loki discovered this and made a spear from mistletoe.

Because Frigg made everything promise to protect her son, Baldur seemed to be **invincible**. Nothing could harm him. One day, the gods decided to test this by throwing weapons at Baldur. However, Loki told the blind god Hodr to hurl the mistletoe spear at Baldur. It killed him instantly. Baldur was trapped in the underworld forever, and Frigg was overcome with sadness.

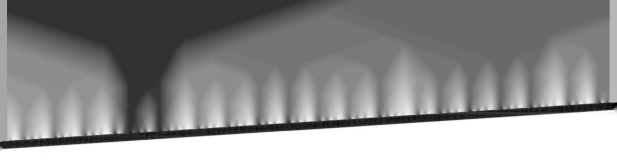

Despite her efforts, Frigg was unable to save Baldur's life.

Frigg isn't always wise and powerful. She can also be sneaky and dishonest. She sometimes enjoyed tricking her husband in some Norse myths.

Aphrodite is the most beautiful of all the Greek goddesses. However, she's not always very nice. She can be **spiteful** and full of herself. Many Greek myths show her punishing those who don't worship her.

The women living on the island of Lemnos are a great example. They refused to honor Aphrodite. So she made them stink so bad that their husbands couldn't stand to be near them!

Aphrodite also isn't loyal to her husband, Hephaestus. She has over a dozen children, but guess what? Hephaestus isn't the father of any of them. Aphrodite has many other boyfriends, both gods and mortal men. She tends to cause chaos wherever she goes. For example, she caused a lot of fighting between the gods on Mount Olympus. Why? Because she dated almost all the Olympians except Zeus and Hades.

Both Frigg and Aphrodite have strengths, powers, and weaknesses. Who do you think is the greater goddess?

Petty and Jealous

Aphrodite is very jealous. There was once a beautiful mortal woman named Psyche. Aphrodite got jealous of her beauty. One day, she told Eros to use his golden arrows on Psyche. Aphrodite wanted Psyche to fall in love with the ugliest man on earth. But the plan backfired. Eros was nicked by the arrow and fell in love with Psyche instead.

Psyche and Eros

FRIGG VS. APHRODITE AT A GLANCE

Name:	Frigg
Goddess of:	motherhood, marriage, household management, weaving, childbirth, family, fertility, the sky, and prophecy
Appearance:	motherly figure dressed in a robe, often blue to symbolise the sky, with young fair skin and long, dark blond hair
Weapons:	magic and sometimes a staff
Strengths:	dedicated as a loving mother, intelligent, wise, strong will, independent spirit, helps with marriage, family, and childbirth
Powers and abilities:	magic, witchcraft, uses magical herbs for healing, power of divination, clever, able to shapeshift
Weaknesses:	her power and authority have limits (she's couldn't save her son), can be dishonest and sneaky
Symbols:	spinning wheel, spindle, mistletoe, the sky

Name:	Aphrodite
Goddess of:	love, beauty, pleasure, fertility, marriage, and procreation
Appearance:	young beautiful woman with long, light-brown hair, perfect body, beautiful flowing clothes, and jewelry
Weapons:	beauty and a magical girdle
Strengths:	power of love for herself and others, irresistible, helps marriages and families, stunning beauty
Powers and abilities:	power of creation, able to protect her favorite warriors, immortal, able to shapeshift
Weaknesses:	spiteful, full of herself, holds a grudge, disloyal, dishonest, and jealous
Symbol:	scallop shell, girdle, dove, sparrows

GLOSSARY

divination (div-uh-NAY-shuhn)—to see into and have knowledge of the future

fertility (fer-TIL-ih-tee)—the ability for a person to have a child; the ability of the land to grow crops

girdle (GUR-duhl)—a belt or sash worn around the waist

invincible (in-VIN-suh-buhl)—unable to be injured or killed

mortal (MOR-tuhl)—one who has a limited life and eventually dies

Olympian (uh-LIM-pee-uhn)—the main gods and goddesses in Greek mythology who lived on Mount Olympus

pantheon (PAN-thee-on)—all the gods of a certain mythology

plume (PLOOM)—a long and fluffy feather or group of feathers

procreation (proh-kree-AY-shuhn)—the act or process of producing babies

shapeshift (SHAYP-shift)—the ability to transform into another form, such as a person, animal, or creature

spiteful (SPAHYT-fuhl)—to treat others in a mean or unpleasant way

Titaness (TAHYT-uhn-ess)—a female giant that was a goddess of ancient Greece before the Olympians took over

READ MORE

Alexander, Heather. *A Child's Introduction to Norse Mythology: Odin, Thor, Loki, and Other Viking Gods, Goddesses, Giants, and Monsters.* New York: Black Dog & Leventhal Publishers, 2018.

Ha, Christine. *Aphrodite.* Mendota Heights, MN: Apex, 2021.

Loh-Hagan, Virginia. *Frigg.* Ann Arbor, MI: Cherry Lake Publishing, 2019.

INTERNET SITES

Death of Baldur
storynory.com/the-death-of-baldur/

Frigg
kids.britannica.com/students/article/Frigg/311342

Greek Gods
historyforkids.net/ancient-greek-gods.html

Greek Mythology : Aphrodite
ducksters.com/history/ancient_greece/aphrodite.php

INDEX

ABOUT THE AUTHOR

Lydia Lukidis is passionate about science, the ocean, and mythology. She's the author of more than 50 trade and educational books, as well as 31 ebooks. She loves writing STEM titles, such as *Deep, Deep, Down: The Secret Underwater Poetry of the Mariana Trench* (Capstone, 2023) and *The Broken Bees' Nest* (Kane Press, 2019), which was nominated for a Cybils Award. Lydia also helps foster children's literacy and offers writing workshops and author visits in elementary schools.